The Little Book of INTROVERTED THOUGHTS

Volume 2

Talisha A. Matheson

ISBN: 978-1-7777453-4-9

Disclaimer: These quotes are the intellectual property taken from published and unpublished works of The Inspired Introvert. All other quotes are credited to the best of my knowledge.

Dear Reader,

Welcome to Volume 2
of ***The Little Book of Introverted Thoughts.***
This book is a collection of random thoughts, encouragements, reflection, and of course, inspiration. So, turn the page, find a quote that speaks to you and let its message permeate the corners of your mind to start and keep the conversations going.

Be Inspired!

Don't let your insecurities *enter* **the room** *before* **you do.**

Today **is**
yesterday's future and
tomorrow's **past.**

When you are kind to *yourself*, you recognize the *kindness* of others.

Not *everyone*
will hurt you,
but you *can't*
trust everyone.

There is a *great distance* **between what's** *said* **and what's** *done.*

— *Vincentian Proverb*

We often *fail*
to see others
showing up for us
because we *don't*
show up for ourselves.

Be *selfish* with your *accessibility.*

Don't let your *ego* be the *elephant* in the room.

Many of our *relationships* focus on what's not *happening* versus what is.

They say *actions* speak
louder than *words,*
but what would we have
if the two
were *aligned?*

Find **someone**
who can speak to your
mind **and** *soul.*

The moment
we *expect* others
to walk through life
a certain way
is the *moment*
we strip them of
their *individuality.*

Respect

is often requested

and rarely

reciprocated.

Listen, **even if you are afraid of what you may** *hear*.

Effective **communication begins when we are** *willing* **to see things from each other's perspective.**

Open eyes can see
disappointments
and *opportunities* **in**
the same situation.

May our desire
to please *God*
far outweigh
the desire to
please people.

Never let your insecurities *ruin* a secure situation.

Sometimes, **we manipulate ourselves into thinking a** ***toxic*** **situation is good.**

A *lie* runs until the *truth* catches up.

— Grenadian Proverb

What the eyes *don't* **see, the heart can't** *grieve.*

— *Trinidadian Proverb*

You know you have *healed* when you *thank God* for the *detours.*

Just because things feel *unfamiliar* **doesn't mean you aren't** *exactly* **where you need to be.**

Don't sit and *wait*
to be appreciated.
Appreciate yourself!

We cannot expect *peace* **when we are at war with** *ourselves.*

Be with someone who *grounds* you when your emotions run *high*.

— *Unknown*

Our *lives* should resemble a *channel*, not a reservoir.

— *Unknown*

We often *mend*
others while
breaking ourselves.

Sometimes
you have to take
your own
unsolicited **advice.**

Sometimes
your *heart* **feels**
before
your *eyes* **see.**

Determining your *strategy* for *peace* is the only game you should play.

Be with someone who *feels* like *home* even when you are apart.

The *valley*
will either protect you
or *expose* you.
Perspective
changes everything.

Calling something
by a different *name*
doesn't change
what it is.
It just makes us
feel *better*.

If they don't make *room* for you, make room for *yourself*.

Fear will
make you forget
who *you* are
and where you have
always dreamed
of *going*.

To *adequately* care
for others,
you must first *care*
for yourself.

It's interesting what *you* **hear when you actively** *listen.*

Never forget where you came *from*. You may end up *there* again.

Arguing is a *waste* **of words, intellect, and** *emotion.*

Adjusting how you
start **and** *end* **your** *day*
will change your life.

You *can't*
cancel **reality!**

Failure to consider how your *actions* affect others is a *deliberate* act of aggression.

Ignorance is the foundation for those who think *everyone* else is the *problem.*

Discontentment
is the breeding ground
for *chaos.*

Consistency should *never* feel like *work*.

You remember
the importance of
guarding **your** *heart*
when you feel
the nudge of old pain.

When one door closes,
God **opens another.**

Never *underestimate* the *power* of your words.

Never allow *yourself*
to be used
as a *comfort* **blanket.**

People desire deep *connection* **until it's time to be accountable, considerate and** *committed.*

There are *people*
in your life
who *benefit*
from being
encouraged but
don't know how
to *encourage* you.

You *can't*
spill the milk
and *delegate*
the cleanup.

Never *judge* someone based on the *chapter* you walk in on.

— *Jerry Flowers Jr.*

Beware of those who *benefit* from your brokenness.

Beware of those who *incite* rage after you have discovered *peace*.

Never **envy what others have. You don't** *know* **how they got it.**

— Christiana (Na) Billy

Don't
waste time *hoping,*
when you can spend
time *doing.*

Unkindness
is often
rooted in
self-hate.

In *life,*
we must choose
our *regrets.*

— Christopher Hitchens

You can have *anything* you want, but you can't have *everything* you want.

— Unknown

Don't let *seasonal* **people slip into a** *lifetime* **position.**

Change **does not require us to** *abandon* **our principles.**

Interesting
how *punishment* and
protection sometimes
look the same.

Comfort **is the enemy of** *growth.*

Respect,
consideration and *love*
are all *choices.*

To consider *others,*
and not be considered,
is a terrible *heartbreak.*

Embrace **all of who you are, even if** *no one* **else will.**

Never fear being *alone*. Fear being strung along on a *journey* that leads nowhere.

When *God* comforts us,
He comes as a still,
small voice.
When He wants
our attention,
He comes
as a *rushing wind*.

Sometimes you need to *remember* **where you were to** *appreciate* **where you are.**

Don't let the *embers* of old pain *ignite mistrust* in your current season.

Everyone **else must take the back seat, with** *God* **in the** *driver's seat.*

If they only call when they *need* **something,**

stop answering.

Even things
that are built to last
require **care**
and *attention.*

Never *regret*
the love you gave but
was never *returned.*
They needed it
more than you.

Remember,
you are *important*
even when
you don't *feel* **it.**

Repeated *fault finding* is rooted in *discontentment* with one's self.

I would rather *live* and face *disappointments* than merely *exist* and fear them.

Don't **allow yourself to be** *bound* **by one-sided** *loyalty.*

People who
aren't at peace
with themselves
carry chaos
everywhere they go.

Your *healing* should never *wound* others.

Note to self:
Why **they did it**
isn't important.
How you *heal* **from it is.**

Don't punish those
who *never* **hurt you**
for the *crimes*
of those who did.

When we *fear* keeping the wrong people out, we *stop* the right people from coming in.

— *@pastorypj*

**If you do it
for the *right*
reasons, for the
right *person*
it will never feel
like a burden.**

Also by Talisha A Matheson

The Little Book of Introverted Thoughts

Soul Talks: 52-Weeks of Inspiration

www.ingramcontent.com/pod-product-compliance
Lightning Source LLC
Chambersburg PA
CBHW051234210726
48290CB00003B/954

* 9 7 8 1 7 7 7 7 4 5 3 4 9 *